RICHARD HARRINGTON

CANADIAN PHOTOGRAPHER

R I C H A R D   H A R R I N G T O N

CANADIAN PHOTOGRAPHER

ALASKA NORTHWEST PUBLISHING COMPANY
EDMONDS, WASHINGTON

Library of Congress catalog Card Number 98-71451
ISBN 1-890356-00-X

Book design: Roz Pape, Seattle
Typesetting: Sheila Raymond, Seattle
Printing and Binding through AIPEX, Inc., Seattle

Printed in Korea

Published by:
Alaska Northwest Publishing Company
101 James Street
Edmonds, Washington 98020

*This book of fine photographs has been reproduced for
this volume in "two-tone black," a duotone process
that is rarely found in the print world today. It is still
widely available in fine printing establishments, such
as our printer in Korea. The results are beautiful.*

CONTENTS

Eskimo sisters share caribou sleeping skins, Padlei, N.W.T., 1950.

Foreword

There are a lot of photographers in this world, and we've have had the pleasure of literally growing up in the publishing world when the 35 millimeter camera suddenly opened up new vistas of opportunity for amateurs as well as professionals.

It seems that overnight, beginning around the time of the original *Life* Magazine, "everybody" had a 35 and was competing with the pros. Today there are many pros with a wide variety of skills. Richard Harrington is one of them.

Starting with a modest folding camera, taking baby pictures for doting parents, and doing a wide variety of assignments for national publications such as *Parade*, in the years following, Richard Harrington was one of those amateurs who became a pro. We rate him a pro among pros and occasionally really great.

Perhaps his most significant pictures resulted from an early trip into the barrens of northern Canada where an Eskimo tribe was severely decimated by starvation. One unforgettable picture was that of an old woman, seated in composed resignation to the early Eskimo code that the old must die that the young may survive.

The old Eskimo woman Richard Harrington was photographing died while he was taking her picture, an old woman resigned to her fate, upright, and with dignity.

This, perhaps, was the essence of Richard Harrington's camera success. He did not believe in fancy backdrops or remakes "in the dark room." He had faith in one thing with his camera… "the moment" when he considered himself lucky to have clicked his lens.

We are lucky Richard Harrington found his moments literally around the globe. Here, following, is a broad collection of his work. You will enjoy not only his photography, but you will sense the wanderlust in this man … a wanderlust that is present in many of us.

Thank you, Richard.

— Robert A. Henning, Publisher
Alaska Northwest Publishing

Richard Harrington.

PREFACE

No working documentary photographer takes memorable pictures every day. He photographs to show life as it is at the moment. He cannot worry about good composition. What does good composition mean anyway. That is what amateurs quarrel about.

Steichen, in his famous *Family of Man* exhibition showed uniquely what a camera is best at—so does the one and only Cartier-Bresson—a given moment, a fraction of a second in time.

What has amused me at times was when I brought photographs back to the Arctic. Eskimos could look at a photo a long time no matter which way it was turned. Once I showed a photo of three men to one of them. He could identify his friends, but not himself—he had never seen an image of himself.

On another occasion, I showed a portrait of a man's mother who had died two years before. For a long time the man studied it, and then said, "Well, she doesn't look so bad yet."

Taking photographs can be a delicate thing—a logger cursed me as I was about to take a picture of him cutting a tree down. Perhaps he was escaping from a wife and family. Photographing people is really an invasion of their privacy.

A religious group argued that somebody might walk on the picture of my mother, and would you like to have somebody walk on your mother's picture? In Moslem countries, where many women are still veiled, you must sneak up on them with a camera. I got around that by buying two burqas (burnoose-type, head to heel coverings) for the girls of the American Embassy in Kabul, Afghanistan. They in turn went to the market unnoticed and unalarmed.

I often wish a camera had a second click in posed photos. Usually the subjects are so rigid that as soon as they have heard a click, they relax and smile. It is then the photo should be taken. In fact, I felt more at ease with my Rolleiflex, which not only has a silent shutter, but can be used from chest level. Even in Moslem countries or in marketplaces where a lone white person is always highly conspicuous, I have taken photos unnoticed, pre-setting distance. Once you take a camera to eye-level, you are almost lost and a picture becomes unnatural.

Once, in Sarawak high up a jungle stream, I lived with the Dyaks in a longhouse. I saw a net holding six or seven skulls hanging from the rafters. I asked the man to stand near them. He became very angry—shouted and gesticulated. I was puzzled. The Dyaks had been efficient head-hunters. He motioned me to the other end of the longhouse. There he proudly posed with a larger netful of his own captured skulls—among them some with dental work of steel—meaning they were Japanese skulls. The Dyaks were pro-British.

In Ulan Bator, Mongolia, camera hanging from my neck, I was stopped by a snazzily-dressed Soviet military officer and his colleague in Mongolian military outfit. "Oh, oh," I said to myself, "here is trouble coming." They pointed at the camera—no smiles—and then at themselves. It dawned on me that they wanted their photo taken. I nodded. They stood together holding hands, very serious. They scribbled their addresses in Cyrillic. I hope they received their snapshot.

In Tirana, Albania, having gained entry through a French Communist travel agency, I was often followed by a policeman on a bicycle. When I stopped, he stopped. He appears on page 53. It was the same during the Cultural Revolution in China, photographing the colorful wall posters. I had to do it sneakily so as not to cause more alarm among an already over-wrought crowd. Later I found that a little fierce-eyed girl appeared in quite a number of my pictures.

Nowadays, for most people, travel is totally regimented—disciplined down to the minute. It is not people taking planes, but planes taking people. The planes direct all travel. With it travel has become more hasty, hurried. No more insight gained by leisurely observing, absorbing new surroundings.

We trust political pundits as they deliver the latest avalanche of words—up-to-the-minute visual news, preferably starving bodies milling around or people shooting each other. All of us absorb, react to stimuli. We are formed by what we see, what we hear. We respond. We are shaped. Sitting on the fence is considered a weakness and unpopular. Be strongly opinionated and you might get ahead—but what has this to do with photography?

The first camera I used professionally was an early Leica with an Elmar F3.5 lens. It was a beautiful, precision instrument and even then quite expensive.

Later I added a Rolleiflex, which was bulky but sturdy. It came with a fixed lens and a wonderful silent shutter.

On my Arctic trips, I found that my own body could keep the Leica warm, although it could be used only for a couple of minutes in 40 to 60 degrees below zero F. weather. The shutter would slow, the diaphragm would stick, the film itself become brittle. Also the metal parts would pull off my eyebrows and lashes, with my fingertips freezing on contact, so often the best moments I could not record. I slept with the camera in my caribou fur bag. Film changing I could do only inside an igloo.

On other world-wide and remote trips, I carried up to two Leicas and two Rolleiflexes—always a spare, should one give out.

For a while I used two Kodak Medalist cameras which gave eight exposures to a 620 film roll. They were very badly made, always giving major trouble. I swear one of them drowned itself in Lake Superior—the strap broke and it tumbled overboard from a lake freighter.

Later I changed to Canon cameras with half a dozen or so lenses. I have never been one to experiment with trick shots. In my darkroom work, I adhered totally to the manufacturer's instruction, using chiefly Kodak products.

A camera-toting person is always vulnerable. Aside from having the cameras snatched from hotel rooms there are other hazards such as accidental bumping, upsetting in canoes, the heavy wear and tear in humid climates, in desert sandstorms and the frosting-up in the Arctic when bringing them into a house. Special camera insurance is always valuable—unless you are away for months at a time.

For years my friends and, I guess, enemies, have told me that my life is a continuous holiday (that's what the income tax people think, too). I, on the other hand, claim that I work every day, weekends, Sundays, Christmas, usually from 6:00 or 7:00 am to 9:00 or 10:00 pm—of course, with short breaks in between—year in and year out. In fact, I've never had a holiday in 40 to 45 years—and I am not too unhappy about it.

A question that often comes up, especially from eager TV boys who want a "reaction" is, "Is photography art?" I do not like to become involved in this controversy—I stay in the darkroom. Certainly it is not art in the accepted sense. A photographer is not an artist. He is a craftsman and involved in mechanics—his medium does not allow the imagination an artist can put on the canvas. Nor do I think an artist talks about his brushes as much as some photographers talk about their lenses.

A freelance photographer must operate economically or go under. A friend worked on a National Geographic story on an eastern state. She took some 3,000 slides. they picked three. Next they sent their own staff members who took 7,000 more. They selected seven. The chosen ten slides made a superb layout, but no self-supporting photographer can afford such extravagance. On an Arctic assignment, they bought Skidoos, chartered aircraft—unthinkable to a little Canadian freelancer. Having almost unlimited funds and facilities—does it really make for the best results, I wonder?

I am often asked what is the most memorable photograph I have ever taken. This is difficult to decide because many photos meant personal involvement. My Inuit photos to me are most meaningful. They were taken under difficult conditions. I came to know the people. We lived together and shared hardships.

To me, many photos immediately and vividly recall a precise moment.

—Richard Harrington
Toronto

EXHIBITIONS, AWARDS AND HONORS

1953   For the *Family of Man* photo exhibition and book project, four of Richard Harrington's photographs were selected. The exhibition included 503 photographs from 273 photographers from 68 countries.

1955   At this date the *Family of Man* exhibit opened at the Museum of Modern Art in New York. Later this exhibition became a traveling show and was eventually seen by over eight million people around the world.

1980   The Anchorage Historical and Fine Arts Museum in Anchorage, Alaska mounted a show of Harrington's photographs called *Faces of the Arctic*.

1987   The Canadian Museum of Photography in Toronto, Canada, Lorraine Monk, director, created a show to honor Richard Harrington with an exhibition of photographs called *Incredible Journeys*, taken from his five Arctic trips made in Canada. Some of his Arctic images were enlarged to five by six feet. Also, a 17-minute video of his life as a photographer was shown continuously.

1992   The Canon International Company sponsored a show of Harrington's Arctic photographs—first opening at the Canadian embassy in Tokyo, Japan. The exhibit then became a traveling show, visiting several other Japanese cities.

1993   Harrington was honored by the CAPIC (Canadian Association of Photographers and Illustrators in Communications) in Toronto, Canada with a statue for "A Lifetime Achievement in Photography."

1995   Harrington was asked to provide some of his superb photographs of the Inuit Natives of Canada for an exhibit in Milan, Italy. Inuit Native carvers accompanied the show to demonstrate their skills.

Richard Harrington served as *Parade* magazine's "far flung" photographer for some 24 years. Also, several thousand articles have had photographs taken by Richard Harrington as illustrations for articles written by his wife, Lyn, who died in 1991. Lyn Harrington accompanied Richard on many of his photographic junkets and the two of them collaborated on many projects.

After some forty years of globe-girdling picture-taking, Harrington had photographs appearing in *Life* magazine, *Look*, *National Geographic*, *Paris Match*, *Der Stern* and *Parade* magazine. He has published some 2400 photo stories and his work has appeared in 24 books including *Family of Man* (1955), and Alaska Northwest Publishing's books: *Richard Harrington's Yukon* (1974), *Richard Harrington's Antarctic* (1976), *The Inuit: Life As It Was* (1981), and *River Rafting in Canada* (1984).

Richard Harrington's photographs and negatives have been purchased by the National Archives of Canada, the Smithsonian Institution in Washington, D.C., U.S.A. and the Museum of Modern Art in New York, N.Y., U.S.A.

A nun is captivated by this pensive figure at the Canadian Museum of Photography in Toronto, Canada. Photographs from Richard Harrington's five Arctic trips were displayed there in a show called The Incredible Journeys.

CANADA

RICHARD HARRINGTON traveled around the globe several times in search of the beautiful, exotic and unusual to photograph, but it was in his own adopted land of Canada where he would take the photographs that became his most memorable and famous images.

In 1947 Harrington let it be known to the editor of Hudson's Bay Company's prestigious quarterly, *The Beaver*, that he would like to go to the Arctic. At that time the Canadian Arctic was practically inaccessible to outsiders. The Hudson's Bay Company operated the only extensive commercial network and, aside from a few missionaries and a Mounted Police Detachment, no one else lived there or wanted to go.

On his first trip he was given the opportunity to join Royal Canadian Mounted Police Constable Dick Connick on his annual patrol from Coppermine to Bathhurst Inlet in the Northwest Territories, Canada. Connick's job was to check births, deaths and to see how the Native people had fared during the year. Harrington subsequently made five trips to the Arctic from 1947 to 1953. Some of these rugged trips extended to three or four months of traveling with the Eskimos and their dog teams, sleeping in igloos, enjoying their hospitality but always paying for his own provisions.

Harrington's most dramatic encounter in the Arctic came rather unexpectedly in 1950 when he was given the opportunity to visit a remote Hudson's Bay Company post with his Eskimo friend and guide, Kumok. Starting out from Churchill, Manitoba, with a 10-dog team, they went north to the Hudson's Bay Company post of Padlei to visit the Padleimuits, Caribou Eskimos. Delayed by fierce winds, drifting snow and low visibility, it took them "five sleeps" or five days to reach the shelter of the post. They were welcomed by Henry and Charlotte Voisey, keepers of the post. The next day they set out to find the camps of the Padleimuits. When they reached the first camps they found the people in terrible straits. The caribou herds, their principal food, had by-passed them. They were starving, gaunt and shivering in hairless caribou skins. Many were already dead, but the strongest hunters continued to search for straggling caribou.

Sharing his own grub box, Harrington found the people eating flour by the handfuls, not waiting until he and Kumok could make bannock, a type of bread, for them. The people had chewed their moccasin soles, bits of skin and dug up old carcasses from long-ago caches. Yet, Harrington felt their great dignity and stoic acceptance of death in a harsh land. Only the strongest survived.

Later, when Harrington and Kumok returned home, they informed the government, and sacks of food were airdropped to the Caribou Eskimos.

In 1987, Harrington was honored with an exhibition of his photographs at the Canadian Museum of Photography, Toronto, Ontario, Canada. Some of his Arctic images were enlarged to four by six feet and larger for the show. The show was mounted by Director Lorraine Monk and called Incredible Journeys.

PADLEI, NORTHWEST
TERRITORIES, CANADA, 1950
*An Eskimo mother gently rubs
noses with her son in an igloo
during the famine period of
1951. This photograph later
appeared in the famous
exhibition of photographs
by Edward Steichen called*
FAMILY OF MAN.

PADLEI, NORTHWEST TERRITORIES, CANADA, 1950
Within the camp of starving Padleimuits, this woman was giving birth to another in an iced-over igloo. She was in labor and an older child lay next to her on the hairless caribou skin.

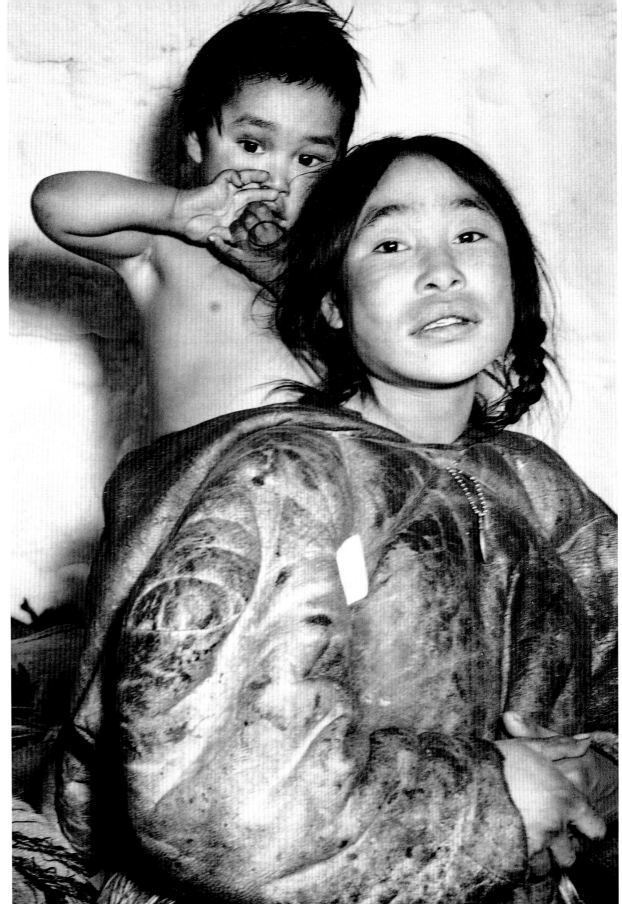

PADLEI, NORTHWEST
TERRITORIES, CANADA, 1950
*A photograph of a Padlei mother
and her son taken during the famine
of 1950 later appeared in the book,*
THE INUIT — LIFE AS IT WAS.

ESKIMO POINT (NOW ARVIAT), NORTHWEST TERRITORIES, CANADA, 1985
When visiting Eskimo Point, Evano Aggark was shown the book THE INUIT — LIFE AS IT WAS *and upon seeing the photo at the left, he at once recognized himself as being the baby in his mother's hood that I had photographed some 35 years before. It was the only picture ever taken of him as a child. He and his mother were survivors of the terrible famine of 1950 at Padlei. Evano became a government worker with an office, home, television, wife and family.*

PADLEI,
NORTHWEST TERRITORIES,
CANADA, 1950
At the Padleimuit's camp, Kumok and I
found this woman stoically sitting in an
old igloo, her hair frosted over, freezing
to death. I stuffed her soapstone pipe
with tobacco, but she no longer could
suck on the willow stem. Resigned,
withdrawn, but still with great dignity,
she died. After the igloo was sealed,
we left, profoundly moved.

IGLOOLIK, NORTHWEST TERRITORIES, CANADA, 1953
Plenty to eat in contrast to the photographs on the previous pages but obtained by Native hunters in the face of great danger. Hunting for walrus from moving ice pans surely is one of the most dangerous ways of obtaining food. Every year some men from Igloolik were cast adrift as wind and currents changed. On this trip during which I watched and photographed, five men disappeared on ice pans surrounded by mists from the open water. Three made it back to land days later, but had to amputate their frozen toes. The other two, with their dogs, disappeared forever.

MELVILLE PENINSULA,
NORTHWEST TERRITORIES,
CANADA, 1953
With my Eskimo friend Kalaut, I traveled many miles north by dog team; he searched for seal, caribou and Arctic fox along his trapline and I recorded the rugged Arctic winter life. Here we share tea and hard pilot biscuits for lunch. My cameras are kept safely warm inside a Kulitak — a caribou fur parka.

MELVILLE PENINSULA,
NORTHWEST TERRITORIES,
CANADA, 1953
With the camera resting on a snow block I took a time exposure of our overnight igloo. The igloo is lit with our kerosene lamp which shows the ingenious spiral structure. Beside the small entrance, closed when sleeping, is a windbreak to hold back drifting snow.

PADLEI, NORTHWEST TERRITORIES, CANADA, 1950
This photograph taken in 1951 at a rest stop reflects the hardships of travel in the Arctic with blowing winds and limited visibility. (Harrington tells the story of how he proudly turned in hundreds of exposures that were shot with great difficulty to Life *magazine. Only one was used and it was in July with the title: "This week being the hottest of the year, we bring you the coldest picture we could find.")* However, Life *magazine's picture editor was sufficiently impressed with Harrington's photographs to give him a hefty advance to go back and live with the Eskimos one more winter.*

THE NEW NORTH—HOLMAN, NORTHWEST TERRITORIES, 1989
Advancing civilization catches up with everything including the far reaches of the Arctic. Gone is the display of stamina, endurance and hardiness of a single generation ago. Now heavy-duty vehicles are used to go to the store in the summer and snowmobiles in the winter by all adults and even children.

*Povungnituk,
Arctic Quebec,
Canada, 1948
I spent a winter with the Inuit Eskimo
population in this far north village
often abbreviated as "Pee-O-Vee."
The Inuit population had long been
accustomed to contact with outsiders and
were comfortable with being photographed.
This Inuit mother was carefully
braiding her very long hair.*

SKIDEGATE, QUEEN CHARLOTTE ISLANDS—BRITISH COLUMBIA, CANADA, 1946
Master carver Louis Collison skillfully chisels a Haida Indian design into argillite, a soft black slate found only in nearby Slatechuck Mountain. These carvings are highly valued all over the world and have become quite rare and expensive to own. The argillite is reserved for the exclusive use of the Queen Charlotte Haida Indians. Skidegate is located on Graham Island on Hecate Strait. Dixon Entrance is just above Graham Island.

YAN, QUEEN CHARLOTTE
ISLANDS, CANADA, 1946
*A few still defiant-looking totem poles
stood at this abandoned Haida Indian
village. They made striking photographs
—their glory departed. Salal grows out
of the carved center and a nest sits
appropriately on top of the totem bird
image. Yan is located on Graham Island.*

SKEDANS, QUEEN CHARLOTTE ISLANDS, CANADA, 1946
My first wife Lyn and I chartered a fishing boat and its owner to take us to view and
photograph the remains of a once magnificent Haida Indian village. This totem even though
somewhat deteriorated is a very good example of the beauty and strength of the Haida
carvings. Behind are the sagging timber frames of a traditional long house. Skedans, an
abandoned village, is located on Louise Island, just off shore from larger Moresby Island.

*KISPIOX, BRITISH COLUMBIA,
CANADA, 1950*
*I had developed a liking for old
totem poles, but rarely could I
photograph them starkly against
the sky. So, it was a surprise,
driving a few miles northeast of
Kitwanga, to find these
beautifully carved totems.*

*EMPEROR FALLS, MOUNT
ROBSON, BRITISH COLUMBIA,
CANADA, 1952*
*Always fascinated by remote
places, Lyn and I went by
horseback to see these
magnificent falls on our way
to a small rustic lodge near
Tumbling Glacier below
Mount Robson.*

HOLBERG, BRITISH COLUMBIA, CANADA, 1952
Many of British Columbia's deep inlets were difficult for loggers to work, but floating communities could be anchored or moved as required. In my travels I found an entire village on floating logs quite a novelty. Loggers and their families lived in cozy houses complete with houseplants. Children were made to wear life jackets if they played on the floating boardwalks outside of the fences.

CATTLE RANCH NORTH OF ANAHIM LAKE, CENTRAL BRITISH COLUMBIA, CANADA, 1956
I brought my Eskimo caribou fur clothes to wear for Pan Phillips' 120-mile cattle drive from Home Ranch to Quesnel, British Columbia. My assigned horse "Hammerhead" was docile and suitably aged. This was one of my best photo stories and appeared worldwide in picture magazines. As so often with people I photograph, Pan and Betty Phillips and I became lifelong friends.

CATTLE DRIVE TO QUESNEL, CENTRAL BRITISH COLUMBIA, CANADA, 1956
Pan's cattle drive pushed across trail-less valleys, mountain passes and over river fords. Only a few miles were covered each day, giving the herd a chance to graze. Here we ran into a snowstorm in the high hills. I was given the safest, slowest horse to ride, called Hammerhead.

VANDERHOOF, CENTRAL BRITISH COLUMBIA, CANADA, 1956
Having read cowboy Rich Hobson's best seller Grass Beyond the Mountains, *I decided I had to visit this colorful rancher / author. Then I learned that Hobson and Pan Phillips had been partners and friends for many years. The stories of their adventurous life together gained embellishments in telling, every time. Here Hobson overlooks his Rimrock Ranch south of Vanderhoof.*

HOME RANCH, ANAHIM COUNTRY, CENTRAL BRITISH COLUMBIA, CANADA, 1956
*Phillips' ranch was two days by horse and wagon from the nearest settlement
(consisting of a store, post office and six houses), Anahim in the Chilcotin country.
Pan was respected and even famous for his resourcefulness. With a home-grown
mallet, he pounds stakes to protect his winter fodder from moose and deer. He became
a legend in his time and died in 1983.*

From Harrington's memoirs:
DOROTHY, ALBERTA, CANADA, 1952

It all started quite innocently. I had asked editor, Jess Corkin, of *Parade* magazine (a Sunday insert of 18 million circulation) in New York, if he would like a feature on what a cowboy does in the winter. He was lukewarm, but I went off in early January in bitter cold weather to document the ranch of a friend in Alberta.

We had fun and I photographed him feeding cattle, rolling a cigarette on his frost-covered horse, doing his washing and taking his weekly bath curled up in a washtub in front of the stove. I took a fine set of photographs back to my editor and, in passing, I said: "Yes, they even put on a party for me, some 20 bachelors and no women to dance with. I even took a picture of the group." His eyes twinkled, but he said little.

Then, on February 24, 1952, the issue of *Parade* carried a three-page spread, "20 Men Want Wives." It was *Parade's* leap year story. Like wildfire the story spread. Not hundreds but thousands of women wrote to the "lonely bachelors" in Canada.

Dorothy was a tiny community. The mail came twice a week by train, and the postmistress, Edna Pugh, kept it in her kitchen. Sacks of mail arrived. She was upset, then angry. Each cowboy from 17 to 70 received armfuls of letters. Two or three local women got upset because the group photo included their married men. "Hey, that's my man, and he is not available," they said.

International wire services picked up the story and sacks of mail arrived from overseas. Women wanted to leave congested Europe. They sent gifts (among them a suit of underwear: "This will keep you warm until I come.") Others sent photos of themselves in the nude: "This is what you can expect."

The bachelors became embarrassed and even bashful because of this deluge of riches and marriage offers. My editor was highly pleased. I became his fair-haired boy, an association that lasted some 24 years. It also showed that an editor looks at a set of pictures quite differently from the photographer.

DOROTHY, ALBERTA,
CANADA, 1952
Tom Hodgson, never married,
and star of my photo story, was
the typical prairie cowboy.
Dressed in his 16-pound buffalo
coat, leather chaps, big wooden
stirrups, with his horse all
frosted, he went about his daily
routine feeding hay to the cattle
that stayed nearby in the open all
winter.

Tom collected his daily mail to
spread it out later among the
eligible bachelors. Naught came
of it.

Living with his widowed father,
Tom did all of his own washing.
His long johns quickly froze solid
on the outdoor wash line.

OTTER FALLS, AISHIHIK RIVER, YUKON, CANADA, 1974
The river roars and foams at a campground 17 miles north of Milepost 995 on Alaska Highway.

Indian grave houses are well kept in the cemetery at Champagne.

CHAMPAGNE, YUKON, CANADA, 1974
A log cache for holding winter trapping gear near the historic Indian village of Champagne, originally a trading post established in 1902 on the Dalton trail.

INDIAN VILLAGE, YUKON, CANADA, 1974
A husky sled dog takes his ease in summer, surveying the Indian village of Kloo Lake, deserted most of the year, but a few Native residents return each year.

POUCH COVE, NEWFOUNDLAND, CANADA, 1950
The curious-looking ladder arrangements on land allowed the fish boats to come alongside where their catch of codfish was hoisted from platform to platform and up to the processing shed located on the top of the rocky shore.

The forty-foot tides in the Bay of Fundy made it possible for the fishermen to use a horse-drawn wagon to gather shad at low tide. However, the local fishermen crossed the desert-like flats with care, as sandstorms blowing across the dried flats were soon replaced with inrushing tides that could reach the belly of a horse very quickly.

27

UNITED STATES OF AMERICA

From Harrington's memoirs:
TARR INLET, (ALASKA AND THE YUKON) U.S.A.

We read in the *Whitehorse Star*, Yukon's daily paper, that our landlocked Yukon territory might soon have an outlet to the ocean, due to a unprecedented receding glacier. I persuaded Al Kapty, owner of a helicopter company that we should fly over the area to have a look. On a glorious day, his pilot took us from Whitehorse to the head of Tarr Inlet. In vain we looked for the cairns marking the International Boundary. They had either fallen apart or, more likely, never existed, as the mountain tops were used to define the borders. To avid Yukoners such as we were, it certainly appeared that the glacier had greatly receded. Cruise ships had come up close to see as well. So, boldly, we made a cairn, raised the Maple Leaf, our Canadian flag, took photographs, had a picnic, flew back and gave a glowing account.

Things went wrong, quite wrong. In fact, telegrams came from the Immigration Department and cables from the U.S. State Department to cease and desist from this invasion of American territory, or else all sorts of dire consequences would ensue. It seems we had planted the flag in the wrong country. A retraction was printed and much later the Canadian Geographic came out with my story—sobered up and corrected. It was all fun though!

A mound of rocks provided a solid base for the Canadian flag raised by me and Kapty.

*Opposite—*TARR INLET, BETWEEN ALASKA , USA AND THE YUKON, CANADA, *1974*
A view of the moraine-encrusted part as well as the cleaner section of the glacier at the head of tidewater Tarr Inlet—and where is the boundary?

LITTLE DIOMEDE ISLAND, ALASKA, U.S.A., 1976
Above—This remote Alaskan community, so often blanketed in rain and fog, is an American
outpost. From it, not only can you look into tomorrow (the dateline) but also to the eastern tip of
Russia, six or eight miles away. (Little Diomede is now a part of Russia.)

LITTLE DIOMEDE ISLAND, ALASKA, U.S.A., 1976
The Natives on this rugged, treeless island must be equally rugged to face the rain, fog, snow and wind. You'd hardly go visiting your neighbors without getting bundled up, even in summer.

LITTLE DIOMEDE ISLAND, ALASKA, U.S.A., 1973
The Natives of this Bering Sea Island still cover their seaworthy boats with thick walrus hides and use these boats at the walrus hunting times. In this photograph, though the boat was authentic, the men were on their way hunting—not for walrus, but for groceries and other supplies from one of the few ships that supply remote communities in the open summer season,

GREENLAND

ANGMAGSSALIK, EAST GREENLAND, 1979
In East Greenland the locals still drive big dog teams hitched tandem style.
On fine days it is a glorious way of getting from settlement to settlement.
Usually several parties travel together.

Angmagssalik, East Greenland, 1979
This wall of snow looks like a large toboggan slide, but it is really a waterfall frozen and drifted with snow. The dogs yelped in fear as the sled and driver descended helter-skelter. The dogs, fearing the sled would run them down, galloped even faster. Passengers debarked and slid down as best they could. None of the people in eight teams descending got hurt.

IRELAND

IRELAND, IN THE COUNTRYSIDE, 1959
We found this tinker with his horse-drawn caravan spreading out his collection of the day, assessing its value. Tinkers can make small repairs, but spend much of their time scrounging items for resale.

CORK, IRELAND, 1959
Lyn, my wife, and I, on a visit to Ireland rented a caravan for ten days. We drove along pleasant sideroads eating and sleeping in our caravan. Having read about Irish tinkers and their Gypsy life we decided to pattern our days like theirs.

IRELAND, 1959
We asked permission to have our rented horse graze on farmer Con Lehane's pasture, with the agreement that
I was to photograph his family the next day—Sunday. In the morning, he trooped out his entire family,
consisting of his wife and 11 children, all nicely dressed. Later, he confided that child number 12 was on its
way. I looked out our caravan's door thinking, "How's that for the pro-lifers."

DENMARK

FREDERIKSSUND, DENMARK, 1959
Denmark always seemed a country of gentle, delightful surprises. I think
it must have been time to celebrate the sun solstice, as men dressed in
Norsemen's clothing gathered on the street.

In Scandinavian countries men and women still love to reenact the past.
Dressed as Vikings or Norsemen, they looked as though they had stepped
out of a history book. They seem charmed by their rugged ancestors.

NORWAY

HAMMERFEST, NORWAY, 1959
In Hammerfest I was fortunate to meet Laplander Andreas Pentha, who, over several days, showed me some of the Laplanders' unique and somewhat nomadic lifestyles. A summertime tent closely resembles the teepee of the Indians of North America. It was comfortable inside and could easily be taken down and transported.

HAMMERFEST, NORWAY, 1959
The Laplanders' reindeer shed their winter coats in great gobs in the summertime. Even their antlers appear as though moss was growing on them. I was amazed by the behavior of these docile and willing animals, having seen their wild cousins, the caribou, on migrations.

SPITSBERGEN, NORWAY, 1965
Opposite—I was able to travel to the Polar region aboard the M.S. Lyngen which brought supplies to the small coal mining communities, trappers and weathermen In this photograph, the ship has stopped to pick up a single trapper with his winter harvest of furs.

OSLO, NORWAY, 1968
Hundreds of sculptures by renowned
artist Gustav Vigeland grace Frogner
Park. These somewhat erotic
sculptures surround this couple who
read the news with characteristic
Scandinavian aplomb.

SWEDEN

KIRUNA, SWEDEN, 1959
When you visit Sweden in the summer you see sun worshipers
everywhere—facing the sun, absorbing the warmth with patience,
passion and total concentration, leaning against a sculpture by
Sweden's famous artist, Carl Miles.

LUND, SWEDEN, 1968
The city's exhibition of erotica attracted young and old, and no one felt greatly upset—mostly amused and bemused.

LUND, SWEDEN, 1968
A young girl basks in the sun waiting for the exhibition of erotica to open.
The sculpture in the court accompanied the exhibition.

ICELAND

ICELAND, 1970
On a trip to see and photograph Iceland's largest glacier, the Vatnajokull, we roped
up to proceed on foot and skis to the volcanic outlets of the Grimsvotn crater.

ICELAND, 1970
A storm began and, at the same time, our snowmobile broke down. It became
our home and only shelter for three days until a plane parachuted down the
needed spare part.

PORTUGAL

NAZARE, PORTUGAL, 1961
It is always fascinating to photograph people and especially if you are not observed.
One early morning I saw this woman near the beach waiting for someone. She did
not know I took her photograph, but I held that moment in her life forever after.

OPORTO, PORTUGAL, 1965
Opposite—Near Oporto this
ancient-style boat floats on the
Douro River filled with large barrels
of what will become a famous port
wine aged in deep cellars. We arrived
at sunrise to drift downriver on this
unique boat, propelled with long
sweeps and an even longer rudder. It
was like stepping into an old
painting—back at least a century.

46

PORTUGAL, IN THE COUNTRYSIDE, 1961
Driving along side roads in Portugal, I came across this unusual windmill with clay pots lashed
to the sails. When the sails turned in the wind, the pots produced a musical sound.

SPAIN

LA MANCHA, SPAIN, 1986
Photographing windmills in
several countries, I found this
one in central Spain, the domain
of Cervantes' Don Quixote.

GREECE

MIKONOS, GREECE, 1961
Windmills like covered bridges
appear romantic and idyllic and
are favorites to photograph.

49

MOUNT ATHOS, GREECE, 1961
Monasteries, located on a large peninsula in northern Greece, are a sanctuary for monks, mostly Greek Orthodox. Women are forbidden to enter. Over the centuries, monks built this spectacular monastery on stony and hilly land. I was able to visit and even stay overnight in Spartan accommodations. Black bread and ouzo liqueur were free, but a visitor was expected to make a contribution Curiously, this view of the monastery has a surprising resemblance to the architecture of the Potala in Tibet.

TURKEY

CAPPADOCIA, GOREME, TURKEY, 1961
The sheer pinnacles in this area are pock-marked with openings and honey-combed with passages. At one time Christians hid in these dug-out hillside structures and caves to avoid persecution. Nowadays they are a major tourist attraction.

ALBANIA

TIRANA, ALBANIA, 1965

At the time of my visit to Albania it was a hard-line Communist regime, so I had to obtain permission from a Communist travel agency in Paris, France to travel there. Nine French citizens and myself were granted a visa for two weeks. I was listed as an "artiste." As a photographer, I would not have been able to gain entry. Whenever I walked the streets I had a constant companion—a policeman on a bicycle. He followed me, stopped when I stopped, and looked where I had taken a photograph. We never got on smiling terms.

U.S.S.R. (Now Russia)

MOSCOW, SOVIET UNION, 1963
I am sitting in front of the famous Saint Basil's Cathedral in Moscow. It is a beautiful and complex structure that no tourist wishes to miss seeing.

VOLGOGRAD, U.S.S.R., 1967
On a tour of the Volga River in U.S.S.R., our boat stopped at Volgograd (renamed from Stalingrad), where we viewed the enormous war memorial standing where the German military advance was finally brought to a halt at the cost of millions of lives—soldiers and civilians. The sheer size of the monument is overwhelming and can be judged by comparing the statuary with the people below.

Danube River, U.S.S.R., 1965
Right—A multi-lingual Russian Intourist guide play games with the passengers as well as keeping an eye on their other activities.

Volga River Cruise, U.S.S.R., 1965
Below—River cruise ships regularly ply up and down the Volga, Dnieper and Danube Rivers calling at ports in Czechoslovakia, Hungary and Bulgaria. The Soviet ships are clean and efficient.

Yalta, Black Sea, U.S.S.R., 1965
Opposite—Yalta is the best-known Soviet sea resort for workers and politicians alike. The water is brackish and few people really swim, but the beach is staked out by the hundreds similar to Coney Island, U. S.A., or Brighton, England.

Yemen

SANAA, YEMEN, 1977
The Yahya Palace, perched on a sheer-sided rock, is a few miles north of Sanaa, the capital of Yemen. It was a military or police post when I was there. I climbed to its top to look over the fertile agricultural land.

SADAH, YEMEN, 1977
Opposite—Yemen has many castle-like, heavy-looking structures made of local material. Very thick walls help to insulate against the heat.

ALGERIA

EGYPT

ABU SIMBEL, EGYPT, 1956
These gigantic figures faced the edge of the Nile River before the
building of the Nasser Dam. The entire temple was moved uphill
before the area was flooded. We visited at sunrise when the sun
shone deep into the interior of the temple for a brief time.

ILLIZ, ALGERIA, 1969
Opposite—I joined a travel company from England called Minitrek and made trips across the Sahara in
well-equipped Land Rovers. I became quite enthusiastic about desert travel. The immensity, heat and
incredibly clear and cold nights fascinated me. It took six Sahara crossings before I had enough. The desert
is far from monotonous. There are rocky pinnacles and some sparse shrubbery, no two dunes are ever
alike, and an oasis is always a delightful surprise.

LIBYA

LIBYAN DESERT, LIBYA, 1978
In two sturdy Land Rovers, we drove southward deep into the desert, camping out under the stars for two weeks. At one time this land was fertile, supporting large herds of animals—even crocodiles in swamplands. Now it is a total desert and only cave pictographs and petroglyphs still depict the departed wildlife. We found many unique rock formations such as this arch, the only shade during the day for miles around.

LEPTIS MAGNA, LIBYA, 1978

Leptis Magna is one of the magnificent Roman ruins on the African shores of the Mediterranean. It was here that the great slave routes, as well as wild animals stopped, having crossed the Sahara Desert. Prior to going, I had difficulty getting an ordinary tourist visa. Only after I showed some anger at the Libyan Consulate in London and said I didn't care to visit his country, did the official raise his hand and bang down an official stamp with a crash. "Okay, you go," he said.

NIGER

AGADEZ, NIGER, 1969
An oasis town built of mud bricks. In these enclosures families live with their livestock and all their belongings. The tower with the projecting timbers coming out of the sides may have some religious significance.

TENERÉ DESERT, NIGER, 1969
Of all the desert regions comprising the Sahara, the Teneré is the most forbidding. There is a single landmark—a One Tree well. It was polluted when we visited. A camel cadaver was at the bottom of the well. Nearby lay the bleached bones of camels that had died, but still among the bones were live beetles ready to crawl up our legs.

ZAIRE

CONGO RIVER, ZAIRE, 1957
When we traveled on the Congo River from Leopoldville (now Kinshasa) to Stanleyville (now Kisangani), Zaire was still called the Belgian Congo and the shipping was under Belgian control. It was an 1,800-kilometer (1,200-mile) river trip. Accommodations aboard were clean and pleasant and the boats were punctual—almost like trains.

KENYA

MADAGASCAR

ANTSIRANANA, MADAGASCAR, *1987*
*A group of well-dressed women had just
passed this girl's home. Envy and
wonderment seem to show on her face. In an
unobtrusive way a photographer can capture
an expression and hold it, almost forever, on
his film. To me, Cartier-Bresson has always
been the master photographer who captured
so much more than a snapshot.*

KIKUYU TRIBE AREA, KENYA, *1957*
*Opposite—While in the Kikuyu tribe area we came across village girls who had recently gone through female
circumcision, a brutal and gruesome operation. We did not see the operation, but immediately afterwards the
girls were adorned with beads and trinkets, and dressed in long cowhides and clanging bells, announcing the
ritual had been completed and they had not whimpered, shaming their families.*

MADAGASCAR, 1987
Madagascar gained its independence from France in 1960, and suffered a sharp economic decline in the 1970s and '80s. Mansions, parks and avenues built under French rule are crumbling. Park benches, where I saw these two men, now seat the hungry and unemployed. The nation occupies the fourth largest island in the world.

Namibia

Oranjemund, Namibia, 1979
Through a good friend in Johannesburg, I wrangled permission to visit DeBeer's Consolidated Diamond Mines at Oranjemund. I was shown a vast, fenced-in complex with special machinery made in Europe of a size I had seen only in northern Alberta's tar sands. Huge rotating scoops cleared the sand down to an ancient sea bed where the diamonds were imbedded. C.D.S. is the major contributor to Namibia's coffers and employs thousands of Natives, from pick-and-shovel workers to operators of the huge machinery. The final sorting is done by closely watched whites, who are constantly checked.

Botswana

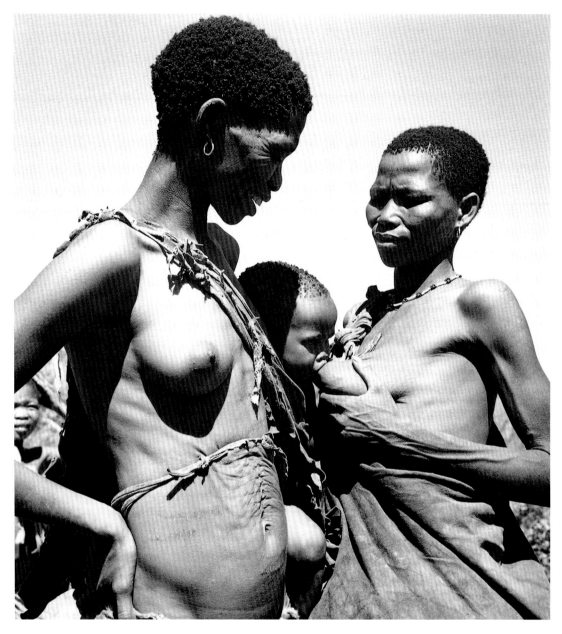

Kalahari Desert, Botswana, 1975
Neighborly cooperation is evident as one Bushwoman feeds another's child. The Bush people often reminded me of the Inuit of Canada's Arctic. Both are so resourceful and fully adapted to a harsh environment, but they still are remarkably cheerful and friendly.

KALAHARI DESERT, BOTSWANA, 1975
All my life I have been fascinated by remote regions and so-called "primitive people." Twice an Afrikaner friend left me at a Bushman camp to see for myself how they lived in that almost-waterless region. This Bushman and his wife cheerfully posed for me outside their modest hut. Their skins were wrinkled, which seemed normal. However, after they gorged themselves on meat, they became quite round for a while.

KALAHARI DESERT, BOTSWANA, 1975
The Bush people are remarkably talented. When their stomachs are full, they take to music, song and dance.
Here, a gasoline container with four animal sinews for strings has been fashioned into a musical instrument. On it,
this girl could play a haunting, evocative and nostalgic tune that I can still recall today.

Pushed deeper and deeper into the arid desert by advancing Bantus with their cattle, the Bush people gather wild tsama melons which contain moist mush—their only drinking water. The men, sadly, have been made poachers in their own land.

SOUTH AFRICA

ZULULAND, SOUTH AFRICA, 1979
Similar to the Eskimo igloos, the round, windowless houses of the Zulus also have a single low entrance. Families occupy these houses made of reeds and grasses.

ZULULAND, SOUTH AFRICA, 1979
The Zulu women dress in elaborate costumes with many layers of heavily ornamented cloth. Even their hair style and ankle ornaments are unique.

BOTSWANA, AFRICA, 1979
Opposite—A large area of Botswana is periodically under water and is called the Okavanga Swamp. Reeds and papyrus grow in abundance, but with the help of a dugout canoe and a Native pushing a pole, we could find narrow channels. It was a rewarding experience to see many birds, among them the majestic fish eagle, and young crocodiles in the clear water. At night we camped on small elevations that had become islands and slept under mosquito nets.

INDIAN OCEAN

SEYCHELLES ISLANDS,
INDIAN OCEAN, 1972
Once remote, this group of islands
quickly changed in character when an
international airport was built. Now
charter flights from Europe bring
thousands of vacationers to enjoy the
beaches with these unique boulders.

RODRIGUEZ ISLAND, INDIAN OCEAN, 1987
*From my Yugoslav ship, the M.S.
Ambasador, I saw this lonely figure at the
end of the pier. Who was he? What was his
place in life, his aims, hopes and family? I
will never know.*

REUNION ISLAND, INDIAN OCEAN, 1987
*On the waterfront of Port Denis, I was intrigued
to capture this moody photograph. Here was a
man bent over in an attitude of despair—
hunger—loneliness or maybe only a hangover.*

AFGHANISTAN

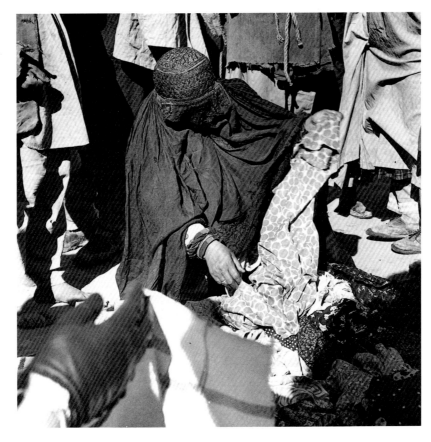

KABUL, AFGHANISTAN, 1957
*Once a woman is dressed in a "chador" she becomes inconspicuous and can go
shopping in the bazaars and markets. She is a respected Moslem woman.*

KABUL AFGHANISTAN, 1957
*Opposite—In Afghanistan I had difficulty photographing women. Most of them wore the
all-covering "chador" or "burqu" and became shy or angry when I came near them. This
problem was solved when I bought a couple of "chadors" and gave them to a young
woman employed at the Canadian Embassy. She was delighted not only to pose but then
she got used to wearing them in public—to escape the nasty comments and hustling from
men who took her to be a prostitute.*

KONARAK, INDIA, 1956
The Black Pagoda at Konarak is a superbly carved monument with highly detailed erotic carvings. The carvings often depict bizarre sexual positions that only a contortionist could imagine. As I photographed the images, a local sadhu (holy man) stood nearby and said: "As you get older your gaze swings upward to the more esoteric figures." Certainly higher, there were lovely carvings of Hindu deities.

KONARAK, INDIA, 1956
Opposite—A detail of the almost countless erotic carvings, now somewhat eroded, seen on all four sides of the Black Pagoda. This is a 13th century temple that had been dedicated to the sun god.

CALCUTTA, INDIA, 1956
Many tourists see the Taj Mahal at Agra, but rarely do they see Calcutta's slums. Holy men and beggars alike sit silently in contemplation and, more likely, are starving to death.

VARANASI, (BANARAS), INDIA, 1957
The Ganges is a holy river to the Indians, quite beyond our understanding. Indians bathe in the waters,
drink it, spread the ashes from funeral pyres over it. If that is too costly, the bodies are simply thrown into
the river. This river feels like a mystical place at all times.

AMRITSAR, INDIA, 1957
The Golden Temple in Amritsar in the State of Bengal has often been the site of bloody conflicts among local factions. I visited the temple several times and was shown around by a local Sikh dentist who later invited me to his home.

VARANASI, INDIA, 1957
"This is how you do it!" The teacher seems to say. "Blow your flute and keep an eye on the snake." The young boy on the left already seems totally at ease with reptiles.

PATNA, INDIA, 1956
Women carry large loads of fodder long distances in homemade baskets. The countryside is poor and denuded, and the soil depleted. Animal dung is pressed into patties and burned to cook meals. There is a shortage of food for an ever-increasing population.

LADAKH, INDIA, 1978
Opposite—Leh, the administrative center of the state of Ladakh, is in northern India. The end of the highway there is called "Little Tibet." Many of the people are of Tibetan descent. A woman rests outside a Indian jewelry shop on the main street of Leh.

Nepal

POKHARA, NEPAL, 1957
I was able to observe this dancer within a temple courtyard. Masks are worn for sacred dances which may teach or tell a story as in a morality play of the West. This dancer was whirling wildly and seemed almost to be in a trance.

KATMANDU, NEPAL, 1957
Opposite—Weighed and found wanting? Well, not quite. A Nepalese peasant brought his two children to a Methodist doctor in town—saving ambulance and taxi fares.

NEPAL

From Harrington's Memoirs:
NEPAL, 1980

I was fortunate to meet Tenzing Norgay in 1979 with his wife and their Lapsang dogs in Darjeeling, India. Tenzing became very famous as the Sherpa who was the first to climb Mount Everest in 1953 with Sir Edmund Hillary. In 1980, I persuaded Tenzing, along with two other non-mountaineers, and with special permission from an ever-suspicious Indian government, to take us on a two-week trek into the Himalayas. Three Sherpas, nine porters and Tenzing were needed to get us up to an altitude of 16, 000 feet (5,000 meters). We carried live chickens, firewood and staples. The trip left me breathless—the scenery and my lungs— but it was worth it.

NEPAL, 1980
Left—Tenzing was always happiest in the high mountains. The rarefied air did not bother him. The bright, glittering reflected sunlight made it impossible to photograph him clearly.

NEPAL, 1990
Opposite—Tenzing Norgay is seated at top left. The party of three Sherpas and nine porters stopped for their portrait at 16,000 feet.

NEPAL, 1980
At a pass, 16,000 feet above sea level, we made camp to listen to the violent thunderstorms which developed at sunset. Aside from physical hardships (it seemed we went up and down forever), life was very pleasant. In the mornings, steaming tea was brought to our tent. Every day we walked a leisurely six or eight miles, with several tea breaks along the trail.

BHUTAN

TIGER'S NEST, BHUTAN, 1975
*Of Bhutan's 13 Tiger's Nests,
Taksang, a nearly inaccessible
shrine and tiny hermitage
monastery, is the most
famous. It can be reached by
climbing a very steep trail and
stone steps.*

MONGOLIA

INNER MONGOLIA, CHINA, 1965
The two-humped dromedary camel is still used to
haul heavy loads near Silinhot.

HAILAR, INNER MONGOLIA, CHINA, 1965
I and two Mongolian herders pose dressed in the heavy wool, ankle-length,
traditional garb designed to keep one warm on the steppes of Mongolia.

INNER MONGOLIA, CHINA, 1965
North America is not the only continent that has cowboys. Near Silinhot in Inner Mongolia, I came across mounted Chinese herders dressed warmly against the wind and dust. They were getting ready for a wild horse roundup. The semi-wild, free-grazing horses are caught with loops at the end of long poles.

KARAKORUM, MONGOLIA, 1965
*A Buddhist priest at Karakorum posed for me with the wind from the steppe blowing his
robes. He had fed me sweet cakes, camel milk and tea. I wished that we could communicate
so that I could ask him many questions. Our vibes were attuned to each other.*

KARAKORUM, MONGOLIA, 1965
My Mongolian guide, stiffly dressed in western style clothing, chats with one of the few remaining Buddhist priests at Karakorum. The city here thrived from the 13th to the 15th centuries under the Mongol Great Khans, and was the capital of their vast empire for about 25 years.

OMNI GOBI, MONGOLIA, 1965
A Mongolian woman wearing Communist medals displays newly arrived milking machinery.
Productive workers have been singled out for attention frequently in Communist countries.

LHASA, TIBET, 1981
Opposite—The famous Potala in Lhasa was the residence and monastery of the Dalai Lamas, the religious
leaders of Buddhism in Tibet, for centuries. In 1959 the present Dalai Lama, Tenzin Qyatso, had to flee
to India because of the Chinese takeover of Tibet. The Dalai Lama remains in India today. In the
foreground, Chinese workers wash their clothing in the Tsangpo River at Lhasa.

CHINA

BEIJING, CHINA, 1965
*While Chinese dancers performed intricate formations on the vast field, thousands of youths in the stands held
placards to form perfect images of political figures and slogans. At a given signal the picture would change,
with never a single placard wrong.*

Right—The camera shake is mine—I was so excited to be allowed unexpectedly close. Below—Usually solemn and remote, Mao had something to be amused about at the banquet on the eve of National Day, October 1, 1965.

From Harrington's Memoirs:
BEIJING, CHINA, 1965

My wife Lyn and I were invited to attend the banquet on the eve of China's National Day, October 1, 1965. I received permission to photograph Mao Tse-tung and his colleagues—a rare concession indeed. I think I was the first foreign photographer to be granted this privilege.

I felt quite shaky because the foreign press had announced Mao dead; having not been seen in public for months, or dying of all sorts of diseases. I believed I had a scoop.

When I left China, I went to see Time's China-watchers and said: "Look here, I just photographed Mao. He is alive and well." They said: "You are wrong. You photographed his stand-in."

GUANGZHOU, (CANTON) CHINA, 1967
"Tazebaos" were tacked to every wall, often 15 to 20 layers thick. I found out these papers vilified whomever was considered suitable in words and caricatures. On one, Foreign Minister, Liu Shao Chi, Communist Party Chairman, was one leading villain. Suspicion and violence ran high throughout China during the Cultural Revolution. I was under constant surveillance by youths who followed me and scrutinized all my moves.

GUANGZHOU (CANTON), CHINA, 1967
During three lengthy trips to China, I learned much of the intense dedication and devotion to Mao's leadership. My fourth visit was only for four days during the Cultural Revolution when suspicion and tension were in the air. The walls everywhere were covered with political proclamations, condemnations and accusations. With my cameras in view, I felt very conspicuous.

YENAN, CHINA, 1964
Patiently, an old, lily-footed woman listens to her grandson read from his school text. At that time only a few elderly women could be seen hobbling along with feet bound in a way that was supposed to enhance their beauty.

TIENTSIN, CHINA, 1964
I saw this girl working in a garment factory—with an old hand-iron, finishing sweatshirts destined for export. Chinese women typically wore their hair in long braids during the Cultural Revolution.

HONG KONG, 1964
Four sailors from the United States Navy on shore leave roam freely along the streets of Hong Kong, probably buying watches and cameras.

BURMA

IRRAWADDY RIVER, BURMA, 1957
Along the banks of the river I came across this woman dancing and chanting, quite oblivious of her surroundings. She had graceful hands and wore a campaign button promoting "John F. Kennedy for President."

RANGOON, BURMA, 1957
A Burmese snake charmer went a bit further than serenading a snake with a flute—he kissed it, or least his lips touched the snake's head. I asked if he had ever been bitten. He said: "No, if you trust the snake, it will trust you."

106

Irrawaddy River, Burma, 1962
The Irrawaddy River is the main highway in Burma. Along its shores, steamers ply up and down
constantly. They offer cabins and meals at modest rates.

MOGOK, BURMA, 1962
The city of Mogok is the chief supplier of rubies to the world. Each morning diggers of rubies and buyers meet, in the small town square. Hard bargains are driven, as no one can tell the final cut quality of the raw stone.

RANGOON, BURMA, 1962
Opposite—The famous Shwe Dagon Pagoda is surely one of the world's great sights. Its gold-leaf-covered spire glitters in the sun, and periodically the gold-leaf is replaced by gifts from visiting world dignitaries and politicians. One can sit for hours there watching the passing Buddhist monks and worshipers.

CAMBODIA

ANGKOR WAT, CAMBODIA, 1956
This carved and assembled head at the great temple of Angkor Wat was totally engulfed by the roots of a strangling fig tree. The head is about ten feet high. This photograph was selected by Time/Life Books for a book cover.

ANGKOR WAT, CAMBODIA, 1956
This temple was literally covered in jungle growth until the French, who took over Cambodia as a colony, removed the jungle growth. This exposed elaborate carvings, many very delicate, that had not been seen for years.

MALAYSIA

BALEH RIVER, SARAWAK, MALAYSIA, 1957
Young Iban maidens dressed in finery of heavy metal belts, bracelets, homewoven cloth and flowers in their hair seem fully aware of their nubile charms. Below on the river are their canoes. The river is the only road through the jungle.

BALEH RIVER,
SARAWAK, MALAYSIA, 1957
Getting water from the river in
gourds is the job of the young
girls. They bathe at the same
time. Afterward, they reach the
longhouse above by climbing
this notched log. Bare feet help
to negotiate the steps.

BALEH RIVER, SARAWAK, MALAYSIA, 1957
An Iban woman sitting on a bamboo-slat floor shucks grain which is grown in small patches of cleared jungle. Pigs and chickens live below in this aerie-like longhouse.

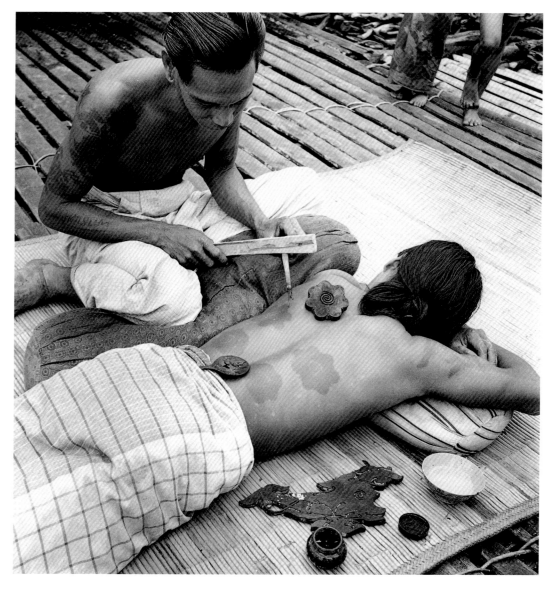

BALEH RIVER, SARAWAK, MALAYSIA, 1957
All Iban male youths get tattooed at some time with traditional designs. The dyes are obtained from trees and herbs. The women do not seem to want their skin decorated with similar tattoos.

Baleh River, Sarawak, Malaysia, 1957
The Iban natives were headhunters until the British curbed this practice. However, during the Japanese invasion of World War II they let it be known they could "do a bit of it." I stayed in a communal longhouse for a week and I noticed this man standing near a bunch of wrapped skulls hanging from the rafters. I indicated I would like to photograph them. He became very angry, talked a lot, eyed me fiercely and finally pulled me to the other end of the longhouse. He then put on his sword and held up another bunch of skulls, which were his. He showed me the dental work made of steel—these were Japanese skulls.

INDONESIA

UBUD, BALI, INDONESIA, 1956
A village dance instructor teaches the intricate steps of a traditional dance to a young, nimble girl. He is accompanied by the village orchestra. Cultural life in Bali is taken very seriously and all participate.

UBUD, BALI, INDONESIA, 1956
These girls had the job of keeping birds off the rice. This was done from a colorful, treetopped, shelter, with clappers which make a sharp noise.

UBUD, BALI,
INDONESIA, 1956
*While working on
my photostory of
these two young
dancers, I observed
they had chores to
do besides dancing.
They first had to
work their way
through dense jungle
growth enroute to
their daily chores in
the rice paddies.*

LAKE TOBA, SUMATRA, INDONESIA, 1986
The village around Lake Toba in central Sumatra is the setting of these ancient houses with steep,
swallow-tail roofs. Only a few remain inhabited and some have been reassembled in an outdoor museum.
In the foreground are stone chairs covered with lichen.

Lautem, Portuguese Timor, 1962
For a week I traveled with an Australian Consul in his Land Rover wherever he could find roads and trails. At one point we needed a dozen villagers to help pull us across the Manutoto River's muddy bottom. We had come to photograph the villages with their unique houses.

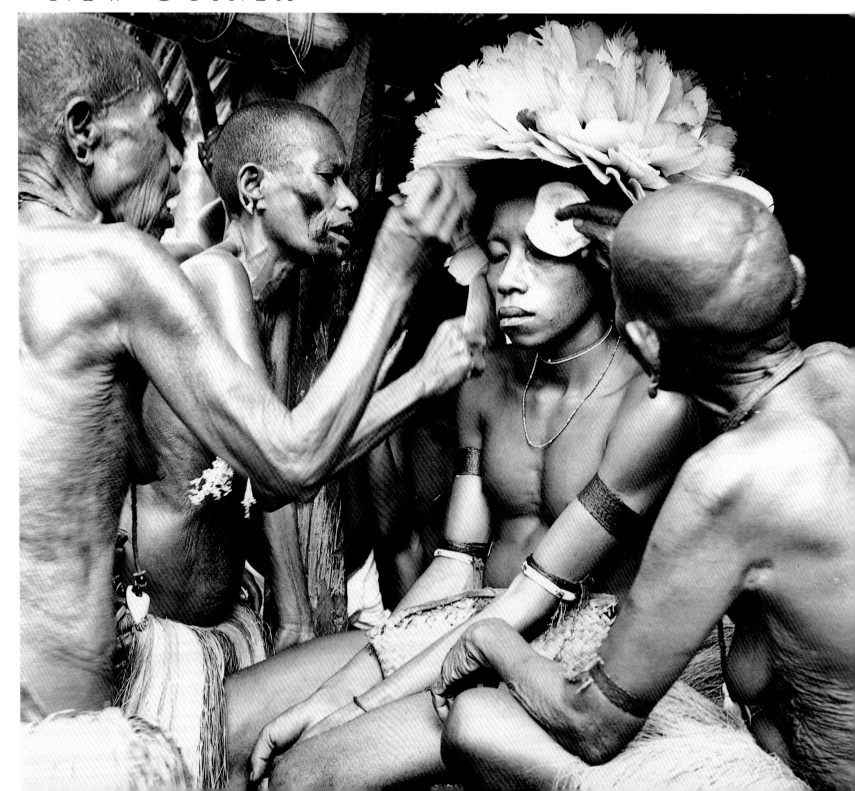

TROBRIAND ISLANDS, NEW GUINEA, 1965
Three village men, getting ready to join the main dance, practice their steps.

TROBRIAND ISLANDS, NEW GUINEA, 1965
Opposite—Often when I arrived somewhere to photograph I was told: "Oh, you should have been here yesterday!"
But for once, I was right on time. The great annual Yam Festival was to start the next day here and I had it all to
myself. In this photograph, three old women prepare a young man for the festival. On this occasion the village
headman would give away loads of yams to villages less fortunate, something like a North American Indian potlatch.

TROBRIAND ISLANDS, NEW GUINEA, 1965
Young men wearing white-plumed headdresses and elaborately layered grass skirts chanted and danced in a
circle around the yam storage houses.

Trobriand Islands, New Guinea, 1965
Young women in skirts similar to those of the men danced in a circular procession.
Some of the women's faces were painted, and everyone in the village wore some kind of adornment.

From Harrington's Memoirs:
Bora-Bora, Society Islands, 1955

The first time I saw the dramatic silhouette of
Mount Orohena, on Tahiti in the Society Islands,
was from a small yacht in 1955. During World War
II, the American military practically occupied
nearby Bora-Bora island, but on a very friendly
basis. During their stay, they fathered about 90
children.

At the local school in Vaitape, the schoolmaster
rounded up as many "American children" as he
could. Lovely kids, they all posed happily. My
editor, Jess Gorkin of *Parade* magazine called the
subsequent feature "Legacy of Love."

While many American soldiers may not have
known they fathered children, some may not have
cared. Others went to die from there. But four men
who saw this feature contacted the "vahines," two
paid towards the upkeep of the child, and two men
came, married the mothers of the girls and settled
in the U.S.A.

RANGIROA, TUAMOTU ISLANDS, 1968
*Every island and atoll near Tahiti seems to have at least one transvestite, a man who is
completely effeminate in manners, speech and dress. Often they were the best dancers,
even leading groups of women dancers at festivals. They are musical and sing
traditional island songs. I gave him a bottle of eau de cologne. He showed disgust, and
said, "I want perfume!" The village transvestite seemed respected, even when raw
jokes prevailed. Tahitians are very easy-going and tolerant.*

FRENCH POLYNESIA

ST. HELENA, SOUTH ATLANTIC, 1984
St. Helena, under British protection, has no port facility, no airport and only one little town wedged into a narrow valley. A supply ship calls every six weeks on its way to Capetown. I had to take a lengthy trip from the Canary Islands to reach St. Helena. Perhaps because of its isolation, the islanders were unusually friendly. It was here that Napoleon died during his second exile.

NUKU HIVA, MARQUESAS ISLANDS, FRENCH POLYNESIA, 1973
The wildest, most dramatic scenery of French Polynesia is found in the remote Marquesas Islands—Hiva Oa, Fatu Hiva, Ua Pou, etc. Often without a sheltering reef and an enclosed atoll. The landings are made by lifeboat, even that being most hazardous. Melville wrote about these islands: "Even today, they remain far off the beaten path." Paul Gauguin was buried on Hiva Oa.

PITCAIRN ISLAND, 1980
Even today Pitcairn Island and its 62 inhabitants (all descendants of the Bounty's mutineers) remain cut off from shipping routes. No plane has ever landed there. The island lies far south of all commercial lanes. Even yachts cannot approach its open anchorage, which is too dangerous. Its own tiny shelter holds a couple of longboats, used for freight.

From Harrington's Memoirs:
TUBUAI, AUSTRAL ISLANDS,
FRENCH POLYNESIA, 1973

On this small Polynesian island, after arriving by local freighter, I came quite unexpectedly upon a major story. I met an American recluse, Toby Klein, once of California, who had lived on the island for 33 years and was totally assimilated into the local population. He had left America during The Depression, had never thought of returning. In fact, his English had become halting, and his Tahitian was fluent. He said he had no living relatives. His U.S. passport had been destroyed by humidity and termites long ago. Klein had become literally stateless and didn't care. His mentality had become that of a native. He lived frugally—a monastic existence picking coffee beans, raising chickens, grating coconut meat, and eating bananas. He could not stop talking when we met. Spittle flying, he cried: "Call me Tony Diarrhea. It's all your fault coming here!" Later, this made a unique story for *Parade* magazine, but the result was disturbing. He received packages of paperbacks and clothes, offers from firms to be their local agent and an offer from the *National Enquirer* to come to America and go on a tour, all expenses paid including suits. Nothing ever came of it. The U.S. State Department would not issue a new passport to Klein, although lawyers tried. So he lived on in quiet hermit style until he died a few years later.

TUBUAI, AUSTRAL ISLANDS,
FRENCH POLYNESIA, 1973
*Tony Klein, the American hermit,
explains his philosophy of life to my
Tahitian friend, Tuteau, in front of his
homemade shack.*

A U S T R A L I A

ALICE SPRINGS, AUSTRALIA, 1968
Albert Namatjira, an Australian
Aborigine, became accepted by
the Australian academe because
of his exceptional talent as an
artist. He vividly portrayed his
thirsty land—at first only for
booze. Later his paintings became
collector's items and were hung in
great art galleries. The artist died
poor, after always sharing his
earnings with his clan.

WESTERN AUSTRALIA, 1954
On a trip across a featureless landscape called the Nullarbor Plain, my wife and I spotted, on the skyline,
what might have been alien invaders from outer space. Locals, however, told us this type of palm was called
simply "blackfellers." My photo agent, Tom Blau, of Camera Press in London, England, told me this chance
photo was seen worldwide promoting a new series of books on science fiction.

Arnhem Land, Australia, 1954
I was told this was a woman-beating club, although more likely it was used in clan warfare. The women fashion baskets and mats from local grasses and reeds.

Arnhem Land, Australia, 1954
I stayed at a kind missionary's home at a remote place called Milingimbi for two weeks. Similar to many other Natives I had met, these Aborigines seemed superbly adapted to this vast, dry hot land. This woman with her tucker bag could effortlessly cover miles of ground in search of bush tucker (food).

ARNHEM LAND, AUSTRALIA, 1954
A local Aborigine displayed his beautiful bark paintings on his stick easel, while standing typically on one leg "to rest the other." The paintings are designed by the Australian Aborigines as expressions of Native lore. This artist's dilly-bag hangs around his waist where he keeps purchases and all sorts of items.

ANTARCTIC

CAPE ADARE, ANTARCTIC, 1974

After an initial voyage to the Antarctic continent on the Lindblad Explorer in 1972, I became so enamored of the grandiose beauty, its stark serenity, that I made three more voyages, each to a different area. We were brought to the shore in Zodiac boats and landed at Cape Adare on a crystal clear night—the sun was still high in January. This is the site of the largest Adelie penguin colonies, some 350 miles south of the Antarctic Circle. An estimated one million penguins came ashore briefly to court, lay one or two eggs, hatch them and soon afterward go back to sea. I will never forget the unusual activity, the raucous noises and the odor.

CAPE ADARE, ANTARCTIC, 1974
Huts built in 1899 by the Carsten
Egeberg Borchgrevnik party, the first
known to have wintered on the
Antarctic mainland, still stand after
many decades of disuse. The buildings
are now surrounded by nesting Adelie
penguins.

CAPE EVANS, McMURDO SOUND
ANTARCTIC, 1974
The historic cabins from which Robert
Falcon Scott started on his doomed
trip to the South Pole still survive
today. Packages of food, machinery,
bales of hay, and the skeleton of a dog
outside his kennel can still be seen.
The inside of the cabin, fully
furnished, feels like a shrine today. It
is now a historic monument under the
care of New Zealand's Antarctic
Station.

SOUTH GEORGIA ISLAND, ANTARCTIC, 1976
Two elephant seals in a typical pose. The faces of the pups have a variety of expressions, generally appealing, but invariably the eyes, nose and mouth drip. Young seals spend most of their time sleeping on the beach, waiting to complete their molt. Dimwitted on shore, they are alert at sea as adults. Molting young seals about 10 feet in length indulge in small battles that are really a test of ramming power. At maturity they can measure 20 feet and weigh 4 tons.

MACQUARIE ISLAND, ANTARCTIC, 1976
The beautiful crested royal penguin, considered by some to be the same species as the macaroni, nests only on Macquarie Island. Between two and three million birds come here each season, some walking up shallow streams to breeding colonies a quarter of a mile inland.

138

STEWART ISLAND, ANTARCTIC, 1976
The yellow-eyed penguin breeds on subantarctic islands as far north as Stewart Island. They lay their two eggs under an isolated root or log.

ELEPHANT ISLAND, ANTARCTIC, 1976
An adult chinstrap penguin sits beside its large chick. It is readily identified by the narrow black facial line and feeds on krill.

ELEPHANT ISLAND, ANTARCTIC, 1976 Two macaroni penguins have climbed the rocks well above the gravel beach to find nesting space on Elephant Island. It has many colonies in the Atlantic sector of the subantarctic islands.

ANTARCTIC PENINSULA, 1974
Adelie penguins come ashore by November/December to breed, hatch and raise their young. Periodically, the parents go back to the sea to fill up with krill to feed the chicks. Going back into the sea can be hazardous, as Leopard seals wait to catch and eat the penguins. A seal is visible in wait at the lower right.

POSSESSION ISLAND,
CROZET ISLANDS, 1981
A young King penguin looks nothing like the beautiful bird he will become when grown. In the early days when penguins were slaughtered for oil, the sailors called the young penguins "oakum boys." The young birds, part of a vast breeding colony, soon lose their baby appearance and, after a few weeks before the first freeze-up, take to the ocean.

ILE AUX COCHONS, CROZET ISLANDS, 1981 Several of the uninhabited islands have vast King penguin colonies totaling a million or more birds. The adults come ashore to lay eggs, hatch them, feed their shaggy young and return to the sea. The penguins' home in the Crozet Islands lies between Madagascar and Antarctica.

McMurdo Sound, Antarctic, 1976
A stranded iceberg makes a dramatic photograph. Shoved by winds and tides into shallow water, it eventually up-ended and split.
In 1990 I saw a television documentary film, and noted that the iceberg was still there when the film was taken.

HEARD ISLAND, SOUTH INDIAN OCEAN, 1981
The Antarctic area is developing its own garbage dumps like the rest of the world. This Australian weather station was abandoned.
It was too remote, too costly to maintain, and the information gathered there was not worth the effort. Now in shambles, the
station is deteriorating in the severe climate. Heard Island, a small island in the South Indian Ocean, is owned by Australia.

POLISH ANTARCTIC STATION, 1981
*Near the Polish Antarctic Station on the Antarctic
Peninsula, enough whale bones have been found
to reconstruct an entire skeleton. Here are the
tremendous jaw bones of a sperm whale. Roger
Tory Peterson, the famous ornithologist and his
wife, Ginny sit near the head.*

HEARD ISLAND, SOUTH INDIAN OCEAN, 1981
*Young elephant seals, roly-poly in body, sleep
on the beach. Hardly anything can disturb
them. They spend weeks lolling about until
they have grown enough to enter the sea.*

SOUTH GEORGIA, SOUTH ATLANTIC OCEAN, 1981

Grytviken was a thriving whaling station at one time on South Georgia Island, north of the Falkland Islands. It was a little town with its own church, cinema and homes for officials. Now it is in ruins. Whaling has long since stopped. Grytviken was somewhat vandalized by Russian trawlers and more recently by the Argentinean invasion. But many of the heavy chains, pulleys and residue of that event are still around.

ARGENTINA

USHUAIA, TIERRA DEL FUEGO, ARGENTINA, 1954
This little building could be called the world's southernmost brothel. The Palerma Cabaret in Ushuaia
featured a parlor, drinks for sale and four "girls" who were available for rent.

USHUAIA, TIERRA DEL FUEGO, ARGENTINA, 1987
The moment I had photographed this dinky, museum-piece locomotive I was arrested by the Argentinean military! They wanted to know why I had taken the photograph and why I was in Ushuaia, etc. Ushuaia is the world's most southernmost town, rundown, dismal, windy and rainy. Argentineans shun it like Siberia. After an hour or so, we parted on quite friendly terms. National pride had been satisfied.

GUATEMALA

GUATEMALA, IN THE COUNTRYSIDE, 1959
This man paused for a moment while I photographed him. Carrying a brace of ceramic pots on a homemade backpack, he had walked all night to reach the village market, where he hoped to sell them.

RIO GALLEGOS, PATAGONIA, ARGENTINA, 1954
Upon visiting Patagonia, I found vast sheep ranches thriving where gouchos have developed their own culture, traditions and style of horsemanship. In an almost treeless country, the cowboys are muffled against the harsh winds, cold and dust.

CHILE

Navarino Island, Chile, 1953
On my first visit to Tierra del Fuego on Navarino Island just south of Beagle Channel, I met the last surviving Yaghan Indian.
Her name was Yulia and at 80 years of age she had outlived not only her family but her entire race.

CUBA

From Harrington's Memoirs:
HAVANA, CUBA, 1968

On two previous visits I braved watchful U.S. Counter Intelligence Agency officials and suspicious Mexicans. The CIA photographed all visitors going to Cuba and Mexican immigration officials gave us 24 hours to get out of Mexico—one was not permitted to land, but luckily a Canadian airline had non-stop flights to Canada.

Much to-do about very little, I thought. However, I liked Cuba, and the Communism there was unmistakably influenced by Latin temperament.

My New York photo agent had managed to sell a few of my photographs to national magazines, but it was a surprise when one day my wife and I were invited to visit Cuba. "Tickets are in the mail," the cable said.

I attended the January 1 event at which Fidel Castro spellbinds thousands of Cubans with an annual summary of what is good and what is bad. On this occasion, it was also a memorial service for his comrade, revolutionary Che Guevara.

As Castro spoke, I angled around, because the tall office building was draped with a canvas of Che Guevara's portrait—a dramatic face at any time. To my knowledge, no one has ever used this photograph.

HAVANA, CUBA, 1968
Opposite—Fidel Castro is the speaker at the January One celebration Day—standing on a dais flanked by his military officers and politicians. In the background is the giant painting of Che Guevara, where only his eyes are really visible in this photograph.

151

TORONTO, ONTARIO, CANADA, 1960   PHOTOGRAPH BY PETER GORDON
Richard Harrington, who makes his home in Toronto, Ontario,
Canada is caught hamming it up with an inquisitive kitten. This
photograph by a fellow photographer made the Toronto-Star *in 1960.*

ENDSHEET CAPTIONS (from left to right – see diagram below)

1. Burma, 1962. There were river trips on the Irrawaddy, the Shan States, Mogok, the ruby center, and at Paduang, lived the giraffe-necked women. They wore shiny brass coils wound high around their necks making them long and distorted.

2. Nosy-Be, Madagascar, 1987. Madagascar, a huge island off the African coast has its own unique flora and fauna. Nosy-Be is a small island off the northwest coast known for patchouli (a plant, member of the mint family. A strong perfume is produced fro the oil in the leaves) and a lemur sanctuary. This wide-eyed, ring-tailed lemur was begging for a mushy banana.

3. Ubud, Bali, Indonesia, 1956. A young dancer, Ni Kunitan, was being prepared for a village dance with a head wreath of budding frangipani blossoms and proper makeup.

4. Rodriguez Island, Indian Ocean, 1987. A Chinese steelworker employed in the vast smelters of Shenyang happily posed for me, but I wondered how this young man would look ten years hence.

5. Hammerfest, Norway, 1959. Laplander Andreas Pentha modeled his colorful and cleverly crafted four-point cap. These nomadic caribou herders are readily identified by their unique clothing.

6. Ogrono, Spain, 1986. This patrician-looking young woman worked in a souvenir shop. I could not resist asking her to pose for me and after some initial shyness she readily consented.

7. China, a southern commune, 1965. Every commune had it sown militia with very serious youths (including girls) going through lengthy drills. They seemed to consider these drills very serious business.

8. Maupiti, Tahiti, 1973. Some of the American-Tahitian children born during the friendly American military occupation turned into beauties. Edna Area never knew her father.

9. Kano, Nigeria, 1957. A woman in the market displayed her front teeth, some of which had been removed and cicatrixes (deliberate scarring for decorative purposes) around the corners of her mouth added as beautification to make her more desirable to men.

10. Fushun, China, 1967. This man was a retired coal miner and was now living in an old people's home.

11. Taveuni, Fiji Islands, 1972. Taveuni is a tiny island whose only claim to fame is that the 180 meridian runs through it. I was fortunate to photograph this young Fijian girl.

12. Muden, Natal, South Africa, 1979. In Natal a "Sagoma" was a fortune-teller and medicine woman. I cast her bagful of little animal bones and unrecognizable objects onto a mat. She studied them for a long time and said I would have a long life, full of achievement and good health. I paid her two rand and took her photograph after much persuasion and urging. For her, it was the first time she had been photographed.

13. Ladakh, India, 1978. This Tibetan-Looking woman posed with great dignity outside a monastery near Leh.

14. Birds Hill, Manitoba, Canada, 1945. My wife and I went to an experimental fur farm not far north of Winnipeg. They had recently captured this adult lynx in a large cage. To photograph it better, I climbed into the cage. The animal growled and snarled as if ready to attack. I took a close-up and got out fast.

15. Kenya, 1957. These girls of the Kikuyu tribe had just gone through the brutal operation of circumcision. Afterwards they were adorned with beads, trinkets and robed in long cowhides with clanging bells.

16. Rangiroa, Tahiti, French Polynesia, 1973. There was a happy, carefree existence in French Polynesia. Many of the girls and boys became aware of their charms at an early age.

17. Mongolia, 1965. In this vast, sparsely populated area I was introduced to an honored mother who carried with dignity all the medals bestowed upon her.

18. Kalahari Desert, Botswana, 1986. Some of the bush people had wonderfully expressive faces.

1	2	3	10	11	12
4	5	6	13	14	15
7	8	9	16	17	18

Endsheet photograph identification